ARS SPECULUM

FOUNDATIONS OF PRACTICAL SORCERY VOLUME VI

FOUNDATIONS OF PRACTICAL SORCERY VOLUME VI

ARS SPECULUM

BEING AN INSTRUCTION ON THE ARTE OF USING MIRRORS AND SHEWSTONES IN MAGIC

Gary St M. Nottingham

Published by Avalonia
www.avaloniabooks.co.uk

Published by Avalonia

BM Avalonia
London
WC1N 3XX
England, UK
www.avaloniabooks.co.uk

ARS SPECULUM
Copyright © 2012 G. St. M Nottingham
Cover Image by Frances Nottingham

First Edition 2012.
This revised edition, 2015.

All rights reserved.

ISBN 978-1-905297-79-5
Design by Satori, for Avalonia.

British Library Cataloguing in Publication Data. A catalogue record for this book is available from the British Library.

All rights reserved. No part of this publication may be reproduced or utilised in any form or by any means, electronic or mechanical, including photocopying, microfilm, recording, or by any information storage and retrieval system, or used in another book, without written permission from the author.

About the Author

Gary St. M. Nottingham's commitment to the study and practice of the alchemical arte, ritual magic, grimoires and spirit conjuration means that he can often be found peering at bubbling flasks or a shewstone – or otherwise engaged in deepening his knowledge and understanding of such matters. His practices also draw on the work of the 17th-century astrologer William Lilly and the arte of horary astrology.

Gary was raised in south Shropshire, where, during his mid-teens, he became involved with a small Coven, thereby gaining an excellent grounding in a wide selection of magical practices. Following the conjuration of a spirit, and asking it for help that manifested when least expected, he subsequently became involved with a group of practising alchemists. He has a background in horticulture, enjoys spending time in the garden and playing chess. He organised the legendary Ludlow Esoteric Conference (2004-2008), helped produce *Verdelet* occult magazine, has taught many free day workshops on basic occult skills and is a popular speaker at esoteric conferences.

The seven volumes of *Foundations of Practical Sorcery* are an unabridged collection of Gary's much sought-after previously published work, updated and made available to a wider readership at last.

For F M N
Mistress of that Arte with love

Table of Contents

INTRODUCTION 8

OF THE ARTE 11
OF THE PREPARATION OF THE ARTE 13
OF THE TOOLS OF ARTE 16
THROUGH A GLASS DARKLY 19
ARS SPECULUM MAGIA 23
ELEMENTAL INVOKING & BANISHING PENTAGRAMS 45

FURTHER READING 46
INDEX 48

Introduction

We live in an age where we are awash with information on all subjects, and to this the magical artes are no exception. Whilst the student of magic can easily access all manner of electronic files there is nothing quite like a book.

A book can not only be picked up and read, but will, in many instances, over time, become a friend, guide and teacher who has assisted the reader on their journey throughout their life. Quite simply books can change lives and this is why those who have been in positions of power through the centuries have tried, and often failed, to keep knowledge out of the hands of everyday folk. This is perhaps primarily because they feared the power of the book to cause change, and change is what the seven books in the Foundations of Practical Sorcery series will cause.

Today the magical artes have never been so accessible, although that doesn't mean the demands that the arte makes upon the practitioner have been lessened in any way. While the arte is, in principle, for all, not everyone will have the self-discipline, the will and the imagination to succeed therein. However for those who do have these basic attributes or are prepared to acquire them there is much to be gained from the practice of magic in all levels of life. For many people their ingress into the arte will be by books, and the exploration of and working with the information they contain. There is nothing like experience even if your magic proves less successful than hoped for: there is no such thing as failure in magic, because every experience will, at the very least, teach the practitioner something, even if it's just to try harder next time!

Of course some will have access to a magical group and the knowledge and collective experience to be found therein; but for many this will not be the case. Magical groups regardless of hue by and large have much to commend them, but not all of them do. I have in the past been approached by people who have gone through a coven system yet then been led to ask me to help them practice and study magic. It seemed their coven did not in fact practice the arte; which left me wondering what was it that they did do. I am aware of similar approaches made to other magical practitioners, which has left me concluding that some magical groups and covens can actually be detrimental to an individual's magical development and understanding - although this is certainly not the case with all by any means.

Foundations of Practical Sorcery goes some way to rectifying this deficit in any student's magical life. They offer clear magical instruction and accounts of magical acts to be performed, thus making the arte easily accessible. The methods and techniques presented are all based upon my own personal knowledge and experience which goes back over forty years, methods and techniques that have worked successfully for me and will do so for any reader who applies them accordingly.

In many ways I was fortunate, during the autumn of 1972, to meet a magical practitioner who taught me much regarding the arte, generously affording me the run of their magical library as well. Having been schooled extensively in magical knowledge from my mid teen years I consider myself to have been extremely fortunate and lucky to have had many experiences not easily available to many people. Thus the present Foundations of Practical Sorcery series is the distillation of four decades of successful magical workings.

Each of the seven volumes gives a clear account and rendition of one or another area of magical instruction that I have received and have been taught. They are presented to the reader in a clear and workable style which will provide them with a concise and firm foundation, allowing the serious magical student to explore the Western Magical Tradition, the inheritance of us all.

Gary St. M. Nottingham, February 2015

Gary St. M. Nottingham

CHAPTER ONE

Of the Arte

The magic of mirrors, whether the reflecting surface of a looking glass or the image that is seen in a woodland pool has always been a magic that appeals to the deeps of the human psyche. The myths and superstitions of humanity have invested the mirror with a magic of its own and it has become a powerful symbol in man's thoughts. This can be seen when we consider how mirrors appear in the myths and stories of humanity. For example, in classical mythology, Vulcan is the owner of a mirror that can tell past, present and all that is to come; the mirror of Merlin which gave warnings of treason and in Chaucer's Canterbury Tales we find the mirror of Cambuscan which foretold misfortune.

Perhaps the earliest mirrors would have been lakes and pools, particularly when they beheld the reflection of the full moon within them: then with the blessings of the Lunar Goddess herself the future could be foretold and the past revisited as well as the present known. For the moon, like the sun, sees all, and nothing can be hidden from her gaze. Yet in some cultures the reflection was seen as the soul of the person and that damage to the person could be inflicted by the working of water spirits should you see your image reflected within a pool. In classical times the use of mirrors in divination was known as catoptromancy and was practiced by skryers and seers of the arte. This was more apparent with the development of mirrors of polished silver and bronze in the ancient world. One popular method of divination when a person was sick was to dip the mirror in a bowl of water and hold the mirror up to their face, if the image was distorted then the person would not get better, if however the image was clear then they would shortly regain their health.

Probably the greatest act of skrying, which is the term of arte that is used for divining, or communicating with spirits that are conjured into the mirror or shewstone, must be the partnership of Dee and Kelley; this is too well documented for me to dwell too deeply thereon. The duo, Dee the conjuror, and Kelley the seer, gave birth to a complete system of magic based upon their communications with various spirits that appeared to Kelley in the shewstone over several years; their shewstone can still be seen in the British Museum in London.

The use of mirrors to deflect the powers of the evil eye has been very common in Europe, and this can be seen with the use of witch balls, which are hung in the window, to reflect back any bad vibe to the sender and are a reminder of this practice. In Italy it has been a practice to smear a mirror with a toxic substance then glare malevolently at the surface and then catch the image of the person that is being cursed. By the same token to catch the image of two dogs who are copulating and then show the mirror to someone whom the individual is intent on seducing had been used as a method from classical times. Methods of mirror divination from the past can be seen in the old practice of skrying into a mirror at All Hallows' Eve, sometimes known as Hollandtide, whereby the image of the person whom the skryer is destined to marry will appear, this had to be done with the reflection of the moon in the looking glass.

> *The nature of the inner world of the mirror can be seen in Lewis Carroll's story of Alice Through the Looking Glass where everything is in a contradictory world, with Alice walking backwards to the Queen and the Queen screams before her finger has been pricked. With Snow White the mirror cannot lie, even if the truth is unwelcome.*

Yet the mirror is not always benign, as can be seen in the Greek legend of Narcissus who falls in love with his image in the water and has remained the symbol of self love ever since. Perhaps any malignancy is simply the reflection of that which is in the soul of the person?

CHAPTER TWO

Of the Preparation of the Arte

Everyone has some clairvoyant faculty, with some people it is more developed than others, and the arte would not be the arte if it was unable to help develop it further. One way that is simple and can be used regularly without any observation or acknowledgement by anybody else, is the use of simple repetition of the fact that one's clairvoyant sense is becoming stronger each day. The simple repeating of a statement that clearly states the desired effect, and is repeated regularly in groups of three, will in time bring their potencies into manifestation.

For example a good time to use your statement of magical intent is when you are lying in bed and going to sleep and again as soon as you awake; this can be repeated if you wake up in the night. The statement must be kept short and to the point, no need to repeat your life's history, the subconscious knows it better then you do!

> *A statement such as 'I am clairvoyant: My powers of clairvoyance are strong.' A declaration of that which you want to be a fact must be said as if it is, and not some statement of wishful thinking. Such an approach will get nowhere with your subconscious. If this is regularly repeated and one has utmost faith in the outcome, then it will come to pass; it will also be useful to repeat it at regular times during the day as well. How long this will take to work is like asking how long a piece of string is, but it will work sooner rather than later; and then its' success will engender a stronger faith which will grant a certain knowledge that such simple spell workings are effective and thus successful.*

Another method, other than outright ritual workings, is the use of simple fluid condensers that are based on the herb eyebright, this used with meditation can help to open the magical eyes to the subtle levels. For this you will need to gather the herb eyebright. As it is solar, you should ideally gather it on a Sunday or when the moon favours the sun would also be a good time astrologically. Whether you buy the herb or not you will need to work on the full moon.

Place a handful of the herb in a clean jar and pour over it some cooled boiled water. Do not use tap water; filtered rain water or bottled water will be suitable for this working. Take a piece of hazel wood that is not green and set light to it, when burning, place it in the eyebright infusion. This will add the fire element, which governs the eyes. This infusion will now need to be strained through a clean cloth placing the jar somewhere warm for a week and again strain. Keep it cool in the fridge until it is used.

Take two pads of cotton wool and soak in the fluid, then whilst lying down place them on your closed eyes. As you lie in this position visualise that your eyes are filling up with a white light as you breathe in, and that this light is promoting the opening of your eyes to the unseen worlds around you. This work could be performed in conjunction with the previous workings. Over time this work will improve your clairvoyant abilities.

Another herbal working that will be found to be useful is the magical use of mugwort. If you have some knowledge of spagyrics and alchemy you will know how to prepare an Ens of mugwort, which again if taken with intent and part of a working as suggested will also help to develop this faculty.

A good practice and one that will need regular practice to gain any benefit from is simply sitting still and holding the mind blank; this is not easy and does take some effort to be able to hold the mind still for any length of time, as one's thoughts like chattering monkeys keep breaking through; but persevere and you will succeed. Watching the second hand of a clock crawl around the clock face as you hold the mind still will help to let the mind focus on a mirror like surface; this will be found useful for skrying.

So where do the images come from and are they real? This is one area where Jung and the occult can agree upon, that there is a vast untapped level of existence that he referred to as the Unconscious. This, Jung declared, was a level of existence that was beyond the consciousness of the everyday, and was something that we all shared. Dion Fortune suggested that the Unconscious equated with the Kabbalistic levels of Yesod and were thus governed by the moon, and it is at this level that we are working when we are using mirrors for occult works.

The mirror becomes the reflective surface with which the skryer perceives the currents that flow through subtle levels via their own subconscious, hence the stilling of the mind which will then allow the imagery to appear. However it is the interacting with this imagery that in itself is something of an arte, as it is not always clear what it is that is being shown to the skryer. Whilst some will use drug-induced states to skry I would question their use; as I would suggest that the imagery that is produced through the development of the clairvoyant faculty is not only more reliable but it is the power that the individual is trying to develop and thus we are after a magical experience rather than a chemical one. However if you wish to take drugs then that is your business, I would simply question their value in the development of magical potencies, others will have their own opinions upon this matter.

CHAPTER THREE

Of the Tools of Arte

The speculum can take several forms, it can be a crystal ball, a mirror that has been suitably prepared or even a bowl of black ink; all of these will work. The mirror of arte can be created by using a piece of obsidian that is about three inches in diameter, or you can use clock glass about the same size. If you do use a clock glass then you must spray the concave surface with black paint to create a mirror-like surface when it is viewed from the convex side. Mirrors such as this can be set in a wooden frame and have various names of power engraved or painted around the edge.

However you do not want to overdo it with a design as it will distract your attention when skrying. With the mirror you will need to wash it first before use in consecrated salt water, it is also useful to add some mugwort to the water to steep in it for a while.

The paint that you use to spray the concave surface of the glass will need to have some fluid condenser sprinkled upon it before it dries as this will help to hold magical currents that are present in the mirror when it is in use. If you are using black ink or water that is coloured black by ink then you will need to pour a few drops of the fluid condenser into the liquid to help charge it and make it receptive to skrying. If you are using a crystal ball then that too will need to be washed in the consecrated water and sprinkled with the fluid condenser. This does not need to be performed every time that it is used and will only need to be done once as part of its consecration. Also the mirror or crystal ball will benefit from being left out under the rays of the full moon, but it will need to be brought in and put away before sunrise. When not in use the mirror or shewstone must be covered up and kept out of sunlight and the view of the profane.

The making of fluid condensers and their magic really deserve a book to themselves, however their creation can be easily performed. If you have some knowledge of the alchemical process you will find it useful in creating this magical aid; however it is not necessary to be conversant with such mysteries to gain the benefit of this.

> I have outlined their confection in Liber Noctis and Ars Geomantica, so there is little for me to say with this current work concerning their manufacture and I refer the reader to these texts for further information. The mirror or shewstone will need to be consecrated with a rite of your own devising, one that is based upon the symbology of the moon would be appropriate. A silk cloth is ideal to cover the mirror with afterwards, as it will insulate the mirror from adverse energies, and will keep it separate from the everyday world.

A RITE OF CONSECRATION:

Having created your mirror of arte or acquired a shewstone for your work, wait until the night of the full moon. Use a basic altar that is laid with a white or purple cloth, purple will be equally good as it is the colour of the Qabalistic Sephira of Yesod and thus equates with the moon. You will need two white candles or again purple for the reasons stated. You will need also a suitable incense and a chalice of consecrated water as the arte demands. Having washed and cleansed yourself, perform the Lesser Banishing Ritual of the Pentagram (LBRP).

Facing the direction that the moon is in address your invocation to that quarter:

> 'In and by the mighty name of SHADDAI EL CHAI and of the holy archangel Gabriel
> O Ye mighty forces of Levanah, the moon
> I summon thee by the might of the Holy Names that govern the realms of Foundation!
> Be thou attentive unto my holy will!'

Trace the following invoking hexagram of Luna over the altar:

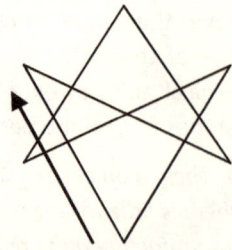

Now take the mirror and sprinkle with water saying;

> 'Let all malignancy and hindrance be cast out so that only good may enter herein.'

Hold it in the rising incense smoke and declare;

> 'By the might of the Holy Name SHADDAI EL CHAI
> Almighty Living God
> I bless, consecrate and dedicate thee that thou shalt be a true mirror of arte showing me that according unto my will.
> Furthermore thou will be a true aid in all acts of magic that I will.'

The mirror must now be wrapped up in a silken cloth to protect it from adverse currents. Close the working by giving thanks to the energies that have been summoned and close with the LBRP.

The mirror will need to be left out and exposed to the moonlight, but it must be retrieved before sunrise and kept safe from the sight of others. If you cannot leave it outside then leave it in a window where it can catch some of the moon's light. Periodically it will be found useful to expose the mirror to the moonlight.

Whilst the rite that is given will be sufficient for this work, if one feels the need to create something else that is in keeping with one's own magical perceptions then do so. Magical ritual can be as complex or not as one's sense of the arte demands, but the will and intent must always be paramount; this is of great importance for without it your magic, regardless of purpose will not work.

CHAPTER FOUR

Through a Glass Darkly

Skrying is a magical arte, that will take some development for the majority of people who wish to explore this magical practice. As with any talent some will be better at it than others. However do not give up if perceptions are not awoken immediately, for these things can and will take time to develop. For the imagery to arise in the shewstone the right frame of mind must be engaged. A stilled mind that is untroubled like the surface of a mill pond is ideal. If you are seeking answers to a particular question then it will be found useful to spend some time beforehand in meditation upon the matter that you wish to seek an answer to.

The room must have subdued lighting, candle light is ideal but try not to get the reflection of the candle in the mirror as this can distract you from your purpose. Incense will be found to be useful, and a lunar incense will suffice. Such as the following:

On a waxing moon collect if possible on a lunar day and hour the following herbs,

Mugwort (herb): Jasmine (oil): Aloes (resin): White Sandal (rare) or Frankincense (grains): Wait until the full moon, and after using invocations to the lunar realms, grind the gums and chop the herbs finely so that they will bind readily together. Then combine it with a little of the jasmine oil, just enough to bind the incense, do not over do it as you do not need the scent of jasmine to dominate the working. Store this in a clean dark jar or similar receptacle. The confecting of incense is an arte in itself.

When using the mirror do not use music as part of your rite as you will find that it will be too distracting and this will impair your concentration.

The use of invocations prior to skrying will be helpful to concentrate your intent, and invocations can be formed from words of your own choosing. If you can pronounce them in rhyming couplets, then this will be more effective as they will be easily taken up by the deeps of your mind. However you must keep them simple and to the point for the best results so that your intent can be focused sharply. Let the working take place facing north if possible, the traditional place of power. You will need to be seated comfortably and you must make sure that you will not be disturbed as this will break your concentration and the flow between the unseen worlds and your own.

You may perhaps wait several times before anything happens, so do not be dismayed. Gently the doors of perception will open and symbols and impressions will arise in the mirror, and even clear visions too. There is an arte to the interpretation of symbols and you will duly arrive at your own interpretations of them when they occur. Sometimes it is only impressions that you will receive and these in themselves can be quite revealing and are not to be dismissed outright. However you will need to keep some clarity of mind regarding their meanings and do not go too overboard until you have some experience of that which they are trying to say to you, and this will only come through experience. Therefore do not be too dismayed if you are sometimes wrong in your prognostications, as everyone has off days to contend with.

Because this is a lunar arte you will be more successful on a waxing moon with your visions and a full moon will be most potent for the arte, that is not to say that you could not work any other time should the need arise. However you will find that these times are easier to work with as the lunar tides are with you.

As well as performing acts of divination, the mirror can also be used in magical workings whereby entities can be summoned to the speculum and directed accordingly. Also the speculum is a versatile magical tool that can be successfully used in simple elemental workings. It can be used to influence events, people or situations and it can also be a useful tool to protect homes or rooms from malign influences. It is not just a tool for skrying.

RITES OF SEEING

The full moon is the best time for the arte to be performed, also when the moon travels through the watery signs of the zodiac, Cancer, Scorpio and Pisces, particularly when the moon is waxing from new to full. But of course sometimes events arise where it is not desirable to wait and one must do what one can; but these will be found through experience to be the optimum times.

Let the altar face north, the place of power if you are working within a witchcraft formula, otherwise face east if you are working within the framework of Western Ritual magic. Despite points in common both of these magical approaches are different and they depend on one's magical attitudes. The altar will be plainly decked in white or purple, both these colours are lunar. Place the shewstone or the speculum on the altar top between two white candles.

These candles must be the only lighting in the room, therefore close any curtains, this will also help to shut out any external noises and do not forget to turn off the phone. In front of the mirror let a small censer burn the lunar perfumes, either the formula that has been given or use frankincense as a general incense. Rites of skrying may be as complex as one's sense of the arte demands with the use of full ritual procedures; they can also be quite simple to perform too. The primary concern is generating a receptive mind for the arte to unfold. A short meditation prior to the working will be helpful as will invocations and prayers to lunar deities. If you are working in the western tradition then perform the LBRP to help clear any psychic intrusions. Follow this with a prayer to divinity and invocations of the lunar Archangel Gabriel.

Let the incense rise gently in front of the mirror and say:

> 'Ebb & Flow Ebb & Flow
> Show me want I want to know
> Let the doors between the seen and the unseen be open to me.
> Let (state purpose) manifest within the shewstone as I do will.'

Trace an invoking hexagram of the moon over the shewstone or speculum. Gaze into the mirror, do not strain to see, let the mind settle with the calm of the undisturbed mill pond stealing over your thoughts, and wait. This can be the difficult bit as you gaze rather than stare into the shewstone or speculum. Some will receive results first time, others will have to persevere and perhaps come to this point several times before the doors open and then perhaps just a little, for this is an arte and the 'spirit will bloweth where it listeth.'

Maybe you will receive clear visions of that which you wish to know, or perhaps symbols from which you will have to interpret the meaning; sometimes they can be impressions that you receive. However the communications manifest, they will all be valid, and you must take note and not dismiss them as fancies, as time will tell what it is that they are saying to you and how true they are.

When you have finished close with the banishing lunar hexagram and give thanks to those energies that have harkened to your will and answered accordingly. Record your experiences and have something to eat and drink to close down your psychic senses, then clear away. Note any dreams that may occur that night as sometimes the clairvoyant faculties will pick up on themes that have been stirred up in the deeps of your psyche.

CHAPTER FIVE

Ars Speculum Magia

The magical mirror can be used for various acts of magical endeavour and not just for the arte of skrying. It is a useful magical tool for working with elemental energies, binding rituals and for summoning spirits. The summoning of spirits is rather a specialist magical skill and not one that can be dealt with lightly, I have covered something of this magical arte in both Liber Noctis and Ars Salomonis. It can also be used to summon the dead who are never far away from us in rites of sciomancy.

A useful means of exploring the subtle levels with this magical tool is to use symbols perceived within the mirror and with one's imagination to simply walk into the scene.

One can also use the mirror for contacting the spirits of any given elemental realm. This can be done by creating a suitable elemental ritual and by using one's imagination and visualisation skills, flooding the mirror with the elemental colour. When the mirror has been sufficiently loaded the operator must then with their imagination simply walk into the scene. The spirits of the element will appear; however let them speak first, after which one must test them by tracing the relevant pentagram of the element or by sounding the God names and the archangelic names of the element that you are working with. If true they will stay, if not they will go. This is a useful method to work with elementals and to get to know something of their realms. Such workings can grant a minor initiation into the magic of their realms and is therefore ideal to work with before going on to work with the elemental energies on a more influential level; such as setting them tasks to do for you.

The mirror can also be used to bind people or situations, this can be done simply by seeing in the mirror that which one wishes to bind. By using a cord that has been looped, the situation must be seen through the loop and, as you recite a spell that describes your will, pull the cord tight so that the scene is bound in the resultant knot in the cord. Such magics can quite easily be used for elemental or planetary magic, according to one's will, and can be complex or not according to one's sense of the arte.

The mirror can be used to influence rooms or protect a home from undesirable elements. If the mirror is charged aright, its power will flow throughout the designated area that you have marked down for it to effect. This can be used for attracting or banishing from your home or any given area that which you wish. The mirror can also be used as a means to influence one's self and to promote attitudes or attributes within one's being. This can be done by flooding the mirror with energies and sitting in front of it for several minutes on a daily basis and absorbing them as they gently radiate out of the mirror. The use of mirrors for magical work is simply limited by one's imagination.

All work is best started with the Lesser Banishing Ritual of the Pentagram (LBRP) as this will help to clear the atmosphere of anything that is not conducive to the success of the work. Let the candles and incense be appropriate to the work: Uncover the shewstone and use a general invocation before summoning the elemental energies to the shewstone. Trace in the shewstone with your imagination the opening pentagram of the element that you are working with. Call upon the energies that you are summoning and see them form according to their traditional imagery.

Instruct them in their duties and dismiss them, then give thanks to those energies that have been summoned, and finish with the LBRP. Whilst that can be seen as a simplification of the practice, in the next section I will amplify it accordingly for each type of working, thus allowing the operator to adjust their work to the relevant element that they wish to work with.

I will use the element earth for the example, for others the wording and colouring will need to be amended.

The Rite of Earth:

Let the altar face north and drape the altar in a white cloth as this will be less distracting. However the candles can be green, or, if preferred, for all workings use white. Let the incense be one relevant to earth, or use frankincense for all works as a general incense. The shewstone or mirror is placed in the middle of the altar and at the back thereof. It is flanked by two candles, whilst in front of the mirror will burn the incense, this need not be too profuse as a gentle suffumigation will set the mind to the working.

Having washed, and perhaps robed, although this is not strictly necessary at this level unless one's sense of the arte demands it, the operator will face east and perform the LBRP.

Then perform a general invocation to the highest.

> *'Blessed art thou Lord of the Universe Blessed art thou, whom Nature hath not formed*
> *Blessed art thou the Vast and Mighty One!*
> *Lord of the Light and the Darkness.*
> *Bless this work according unto my holy will.'* (Or words of your choosing)

Next turn desoil (sunwise) and face north for the earth element conjuration and prayers.

Trace over the mirror the opening earth pentagram thus:

Earth

And intone:

> *For in and by the might of the Holy Name of God ADONAI HA ARETZ*
> *Lord of this Earth*
> *and of the Mighty Archangel Uriel who art the Archangel of*

> Tzaphon.
> And by the power of the Holy Angel Phorlak O ye Mighty King Ghob
> Let the energies of the earth be attentive unto my will!

Read the following elemental prayer of the earth kingdoms.

> 'O Invisible King who doth take the earth for foundation, didst hollow their depths to fill them with Thy Almighty Power.
> Thou whose Name doth shake the arches of the world,
> rewarder of the subterranean workers, lead us into the desirable air
> and into the realm of splendour.
> We watch and we labour unceasingly, for we seek and we hope by the twelve stones of the Holy City,
> by the buried talismans
> and the axis of the lodestone which passes through the centre of the earth!
>
> O Lord! O Lord! O Lord!
>
> Have pity upon those who suffer.
> Expand our hearts, unbind and upraise our minds, enlarge our natures.
> Thou who wearest the heavens on thy finger like a ring of sapphire!
> Thou who hidest beneath the earth in the kingdom of the gems, the marvellous seed of the stars!
>
> Live, reign and be thou the eternal dispenser of the treasures, whereof thou hast made us the wardens.'

Let the mind be still for a moment and as you breathe in visualise that the mirror fills with the colour green. Do this for several breaths and the mirror will fill with the element. Gaze into the mirror but do not strain your eyes, visualise an opening pentagram in the mirror and watch the scenes as they appear before you. When the visions have ceased and the links with the subtle levels have faded, close by seeing the banishing pentagram form in the mirror and the energies fade from view.

Earth

Give thanks for the success of the working thus:

> 'Unto the Holy Names of God ADONIA HA ARETZ
> and to the Mighty Archangel Uriel and the Holy Angel Phorlak and
> the King of Earth Ghob
> Do I give thanks for the success of this mine act of magic.
> Therefore let there be peace, grace and harmony between me and
> thee now and for always.
> So Mote It Be!'

The rite can be concluded by the use of the LBRP. Whilst it can be seen as simplification of magical ritual it is not any the less potent for it, as magic is driven by one's magical will rather than theatrics, despite how awesomely they may be performed. The above formula can be added to and customised, but follow the same ritual pattern, which is important, as the highest is invoked first and then the next level and so on; which is the formula of YHVH.

Another means of magic is to follow the above to the point of gazing into the mirror, and at this point again invoke the element with the use of the divine names. Then you must see in the mirror that which you wish to happen, however this must be in accordance with the office of the element that you are working with for it to be effective. Or one can light a candle of the element's colour and place it in front of the mirror. Then see in the candle flame that is reflected within the mirror that which you wish to happen. This work combines candle magic with mirror magic and is an important modus of the arte that will lend itself to all manner of magical workings.

> The use of Psalms is also to be noted as they are an important source of ritualistic conjurations. Whilst many would consider them to belong to the Christian church and therefore inappropriate for magical use as they would be uncomfortable with their use in their magic, many magicians of the past and

indeed the present have appreciated their power. As the Psalms have been used for centuries they have acquired a potency of their own, which can easily be exploited for magical workings by the conjuror with great success.

By working with the formula given above and adapting it with the following tabulation other rites according to one's needs can easily be constructed by the conjuror of the arte.

Air:

God Name	Shaddai El Chai (Almighty Living God)
Archangel	Raphael
Angel	Chassan
King	Paralda
Spirits	Sylphs
Colour	Yellow
Incense	Dammar - Galbanum

Invocations:

'Such a fire existeth extending through the rushing of air, or even a fire, formless whence cometh the image of a voice or even a flashing light, abounding revolving, whirling forth crying aloud!'

Prayer of the Sylphs:

*'Spirit of Life, Spirit of Wisdom whose breath
giveth forth and withdraweth the form of all things.
We praise thee and we bless thee
in the changeless empire of created light of shades of reflections
and of images.
And we aspire without cessation
unto thy immutable and imperishable brilliance.
Let the ray of thy intelligence and the warmth
of thy love penetrate even unto us.*

*And no more shall we be swept away
by the tempest but we shall hold the bridles of the winged steeds
of dawn.
And we shall direct the course of the evening breeze
to fly before thee,
the divine ocean of movement and truth.'*

Fire:

God Name	YHVH TZABAOTH (God of Armies)
Archangel	Mikael
Angel	Aral
King	Djinn
Spirits	Salamanders
Colour	Red
Incense	Dragon's Blood - Pepper - Nettle

Invocations:

'And when after all the phantoms have vanished, thou shalt see that holy and formless fire,
that fire which darts and flashes through the hidden depths of the Universe, hear thou the voice of fire!'

Prayer of the Salamanders:

'Immortal eternal ineffable and uncreated father of all
borne upon the chariot of worlds which ever roll in ceaseless motion
help us thy children whom thou hast loved since the birth of the ages of time!
Thy majesty golden vast and eternal shineth above the heaven of stars.
Above them art thou exalted.
Our continual exercise is to praise and to adore thy desires
there we ceaselessly
burn with eternal aspirations unto thee.
O Father,
O Mother of Mothers
O Son the flower of all sons.
Form of all forms Soul spirit harmony
and numeral of all things!'

Water:

God Name	ELOHIM TZABAOTH (Gods of Hosts)
Archangel	Gabriel
Angel	Taliahad
King	Niksa
Spirits	Undines
Colour	Blue
Incense	Vanilla, Rose, Jasmine

Invocations:

'So therefore the priest who governeth the works of fire doth sprinkle with the waters
of the loud resounding sea.'

Prayer of the Undines:

'Terrible King of the Sea,
King of the deluge and of the rains of spring.
Thou who commandest moisture which is as it were the blood of the earth
to become the sap of the plants.
We adore thee and we invoke thee.
Speak thou unto us,
thou mobile and changeful creatures in the great tempests and we shall tremble before thee.

Speak to us also in the murmur of the limpid waters and we shall desire thy love.
Lead us unto immortality through sacrifice that we may be found worthy
to offer one day unto thee the water the blood and the tears
for the remission of sin.'

Earth:

God Name	ADONIA HA ARETZ (Lord of this Earth)
Archangel	Uriel
Angel	Phorlak
King	Ghob
Spirits	Gnomes
Incense	Storax - Patchouli
Colour	Green

Invocations:

'Stoop not down into that darkly splendid world wherein continually lieth a faithless depth and Hades wrapped in gloom delighting in unintelligible images precipitous, winding, a black ever rolling abyss
ever espousing a body unluminous formless and void.'

Prayer of the Gnomes:

'O invisible King who taking the earth for foundation didst hollow its depths to fill them with thy almighty power.
Thou whose name shaketh the arches
of the world rewarder of the subterranean workers lead us into the desirable air
and into the realm of splendour.
We watch and we labour unceasingly.
We seek and we hope by the twelve stones of the holy city by the buried talismans
by the axis of the lodestone which passes through the centre of the earth!
O Lord! O Lord! O Lord!
Have pity upon those who suffer expand our hearts unbind and upraise our minds
enlarge our natures Thou who wearest

the heavens on thy finger like a ring of sapphire!
Thou who hidest beneath the earth in the Kingdom of Gems the marvelous seed of the stars!
Live reign and be Thou the eternal dispenser of the treasures whereof Thou hast made us the wardens.'

Rites of Ligature:

Whilst the binding of someone or something may be looked upon as being a practice of a dubious nature, all the same it is a useful magical skill to develop. I would not suggest that you use it lightly as it does work. When the moon is waning set your altar as suggested unless you wish to work within a full ritualistic modus. Use myrrh for incense and if possible let the altar cloth and candles be black in colour, also you will need a black cord big enough to make a loop and to tie three knots in; black being appropriate to the working.

Use a general invocation of your devising to God for success in this operation of the arte. State your intent simply and clearly, with no ambiguity. This is an important point for all spell workings whatever their hue. Now hold the cord in the rising incense smoke as you state your will.

> *Holding the cord tie a loop in the middle but do not pull it tight yet as you will need to peer through the loop into the mirror as the incense smoke rises before the mirror and the candle light shimmers. However before you do this recite Psalm 109.*

> *'Be not silent O God of my praise*
> *For wicked and deceitful mouths are opened against me speaking against me with lying tongues*
> *They beset me with words of hate and attack me without cause.*
> *In return for my love they accuse me even as I make prayer for them.*
> *So they reward me evil for good and hatred for my love.*

> *Appoint a wicked man against him let an accuser bring them to trial.*
> *When he is tried let him come forth guilty let his prayer be counted as sin.*
> *May his days be few may another seize his goods May his children*

be fatherless and his wife a widow.
May his children wander about and beg
May they be driven out of the ruins they inhabit!
May the creditor seize all that he has.
May strangers plunder the fruits of his toil!

Let there be none to extend kindness to him nor any to pity his fatherless children
may his posterity be cut off
May his name be blotted out in the second generation!
May the iniquity of his fathers be remembered before the Lord
and let not the sin of his mother be blotted out

Let them be before the Lord continually and may his memory be cut off from the earth!
For he did not remember to show kindness but pursued the poor and needy
and the broken-hearted to their death.

He loved to curse let curses come upon him He did not like blessing may it be far from him.
He clothed himself with cursing as his coat may it soak into his body like water like oil into his bones.
May it be like a garment which he wraps around him like a belt with which he daily girds himself!

May this be the reward of my accusers from the Lord of those who speak evil against my life!
But thou O God my Lord deal on my behalf
for thy name's sake because thy steadfast love is good deliver me!

For I am poor and needy and my heart is stricken within me.
I am gone like a shadow at evening I am shaken off like a locust.
My knees are weak through fasting my body has become gaunt
I am an object of scorn to my accusers when they see me, they wag their heads.

Help me, O Lord my God
Save me according to thy steadfast love!
Let them know that this is thy hand thou O Lord hast done it.
Let them curse, but do thou bless!

Let my assailants be put to shame may thy servant be glad! May my accusers be clothed with dishonour may they be wrapped in their own shame as in a mantle.

With my mouth I will give great thanks to the Lord I will praise him in the midst of the throng.
For he stands at the right hand of the needy to save him from those who would condemn him.'

Gaze into the mirror through the loop that you have made in the cord and see the situation or person that you wish to bind. State that which you will to occur, if you can put it into rhyming couplets so much the better, even if they sound a little absurd. As long as they encapsulate your will, they will suffice for this working. Now pull the cord tight to catch and bind the spell. Repeat this action twice more so that you have worked this thrice. Hold the cord with the three knots in the rising incense smoke and say;

'As I do will So Mote It Be!'

Give thanks to the energies that you have invoked by dismissing them in your own words. Wrap the black cord in a black cloth, silk would be ideal. Perform the LBRP to close any stray energies that are still present. If you can bury the cord in a churchyard, this would be ideal and so much the better. If not, put it somewhere safe, where it will not be disturbed and let it do its work unmolested.

Such workings as this can be disturbing to one's psyche and are not to be undertaken lightly. Having put everything away, have something to eat and drink, and record any impressions that you have and of course the outcome.

Earth:

The mirror can be used for increasing good fortune and bringing good things into your life that will benefit you materially; such workings belong to the element earth.

Firstly consider the astrology of your proposed working and let the moon be in an earth sign, and by using the colours and invocations that have been given previously summon the forces of the earth unto your aid. Light a green candle in front of the mirror and trace in the mirror the invoking pentagram of earth and intone the following as you visualise the astrological sign of Taurus, which is the symbol for the Earth element:

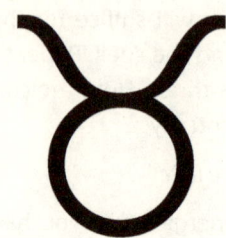

'Let us adore ADONAI HA ARETZ Lord of this Earth
Unto Thee be the Kingdom and the Power and the Glory.'
And the Elohim said:
'Let us make Adam in our image
after our likeness and let him have dominion over the fish of the sea and over the fowl of the air
and over the cattle and over all the earth and over every creeping thing
that creepeth over the earth.
And the Elohim created ETH HA - ADAM in their own image, in the image of the Elohim
created they him.
In the name of ADONAI MELEKH and of the Bride and Queen of the Kingdom, Spirits of Earth adore ADONAI.'

Invoke with Psalm 126:

'When the Lord restored the fortunes of Zion we were like those in a dream.
Then our mouth was filled with laughter and our tongue with

shouts of joy then they said among the nations
The Lord has done great things for them
The Lord has done great things for us we are glad.
Restore our fortunes O Lord, like the water courses in the Negeb!
May those who sow in tears reap with shouts of joy.
He that goes forth weeping bearing the seed for sowing
shall come home with shouts of joy bringing his sheaves with him.'

As you breathe in let the mirror fill with a green light, do this several times. State clearly in your own words that which you are working for in the sure and certain knowledge that it will manifest in your life. See it happen.

When the tensions have broken and the magic is released, give thanks to the element earth and the God most High.

Close the rite.

Air:

This is the element to use when you wish to move someone or something on. It will need to be done on a waning moon.

To help with healing, work when the moon is waxing. This is the element which can be used to help with a trouble-free journey, and is always useful; it will also promote learning.

When the moon is in an air sign such as Gemini, Libra or Aquarius, set the altar as the arte demands, using the colours and invocations appertaining to the element air as have been given previously; set the altar to face east the direction of air. Then face the mirror and trace the invoking air pentagram with the yellow candle, which will be in front of the mirror of arte and state your intent.

'Let us adore the Lord and King of Air SHADDAI EL CHAI
Almighty and Everlasting
ever living be thy name magnified in the life of all."
And the Elohim said
Let us make Adam in our image after our likeness, and let him have dominion over the fowl of the air.'
'In the name of YOD HEH VAV HEH and in the name of SHADDAI EL CHAI
Spirits of Air adore thy Creator.'

Let the incense rise before the mirror, gently and not too copiously, then gaze at the flame that is reflected in the mirror and recite your invocations of the element air.

See in the mirror a fine yellow light slowly build up as the energies are summoned. Now look deep into the mirror and see your will coming to pass. When the energies are exhausted and your will has been set, then give thanks to the element air and close the rite.

Fire:

The energies of the fire element will promote creativity and are also protective in an active sense, for the energies are by nature never still and fire can be fierce. Let the working take place when the moon is domiciled in one of the fire signs such as Aries, Leo or Sagittarius.

After using the invocations for the element, trace the fire invoking pentagram in the mirror with the red candle which will be in front of the mirror and state your intent. After reciting the invocations gaze into the mirror and let it fill with a red light as you do. Watch as your will is formed in the mirror and see it come to pass. Close with appropriate banishings and give thanks.

> *'Let us adore the Lord and King of Fire.*
> *YOD HEH VAV HEH*
> *Blessed be thou - Leader of Armies is Thy Name.'*
> *'And Elohim said*
> *let us make Adam in our own image, after our own likeness and let him have dominion.*
> *In the name of Elohim mighty and ruling and in the name and in the name YOD HEH VAV HEH TZABAOTH*
> *Spirit of Fire adore thy Creator.'*

Water:

The mirror has a natural sympathy with the element of water, as both their surfaces are reflective. Water is a good element to work with regarding emotional matters. Whether you use your mirror, or construct a rite outside sitting by a pool of water, in which the moon is reflected, begin by gazing at the moon's reflection in the pool, as one would use a mirror. Spells and charms can easily be invoked and released using this method. However if working inside then as before use the given colours, incense and invocations. Set up the mirror with a blue candle in front and invoke the undines. Trace in the mirror with the candle flame the invoking pentagram of water and invoke with the following invocations as you gaze into the mirror.

'Let us adore the Lord and King of Water.
ELOHIM TZABAOTH
ELOHIM of Hosts!
Glory be to the RUACH ELOHIM
who moved upon the face of the waters of creation.' And ELOHIM said;
'Let us make Adam in our image after our likeness and let him
have dominion over the fish of the sea. In the name of EL strong and powerful and in the name of ELOHIM TZABAOTH Spirits of Water adore your Creator!'

Let the mirror fill with a gentle blue light as you say softly, but intently:

(From the Song of Solomon)

'O that you would kiss me with the kisses of thy mouth
For your love is better than wine
your anointing oils are fragrant your name is oil poured out.
Therefore the maidens love thee.
Draw me after you, let us make haste.

The King has brought me into his chambers.
We will exult and rejoice in you
we will extol your love more than wine
rightly do they love you.'
'Behold you are beautiful my love behold you are beautiful
your eyes are doves.
For I am the Rose of Sharon and the Lily of the Valley
As a Lily among brambles
So is my love among maidens.'

See in the mirror that which is your will now coming to pass. For it can be none other. Let the energies disperse as they attend to your magic. Give thanks and close the rite.

The Mirror as a Defensive Tool:

Such workings with the mirror are quite simple and they may be used to protect a home, building or an individual. When the moon is waxing, a simple working may be performed by clearing the psychic atmosphere and sitting in front of the mirror, this work can be done by using a dish and filling it with water to which a few drops of fluid condenser have been added. (See Liber Noctis).

Then by emptying your mind and relaxing contrive to see the universe as an ocean of brilliance and with each breath you suck this light into yourself and when you feel sated pour the light into the mirror. You must see and sense the mirror to be glowing with this power. Franz Bardon in his work Initiation into Hermetics tells how overcharging a mirror like this can shatter it, however you are unlikely to be working at this level! Having charged the mirror as best one can, try to place your consciousness in the centre of this light, even if it is momentarily and impress upon it your will whether it is to attract or repel someone or something; keep it concise and keep it simple. If you are working on behalf of someone else then do not pass the light through your body, simply see it being drawn out of the universe and into the mirror instead.

This working may need to be repeated, but this is going to depend upon how effective your will-power is and how developed your visualisation skills are. If the mirror is to have a long term influence then regular charging will be found to be useful. When the mirror has been sufficiently charged place it somewhere safe and let its influence flood the area that it is to be effective in. If it is to work upon oneself then instruct it so. Working with the mirror as such will be found useful to promote a calm and peaceful atmosphere in the home or to attract good things to you.

Finally the mirror is a useful tool in the arte of conjuration and I give clear and detailed instructions in its use in such matters in Ars Salomonis. Basically the mirror is placed within a triangle of arte that has been created upon the altar top and the spirits are conjured into the mirror. The triangle operates as a barrier that contains them, this is a system that works well, but does require a high level of magical abilities and experience, so is not a work that is suitable for the early student, particularly as some of the spirits can be alarming in appearance and the conjuror will need to be in full control of the situation. An account of a conjuration of a Goetia spirit that was given to me by a practitioner of the arte will demonstrate this point.

The working was performed with the mirror on the altar as described and by long and arduous rites the spirit Seere, who is the seventieth spirit of the Lesser Key of Solomon (the Goetia) was eventually conjured into the mirror. The skryer, who was female, and they generally make the best skryers, started to described the scene. Firstly the skryer had no idea of the spirit's description or office that God had appointed it. But they were all described accurately, firstly the skryer became visibly shaken by what they described as the head of a horse that appeared to be coming out of the mirror but was thankfully contained by the triangle of arte. The spirit appeared to be angry with the conjuror for disturbing them, but with the use of the Seal of Solomon and the binding angel the scene settled down, but not much.

Suddenly the imagery changed, the sky appeared dark and menacing. A long column of armed men manifested in the shewstone with a man on horseback leading them, who on interrogation declares their office and who they are. This is in accordance with their traditional Goetia descriptions. By now the skryer was feeling the strain and the spirit was given their instructions in a clear manner, and was then Licensed to Depart to their realms and habitations, causing no fear nor harm to any. This was done as the arte demands and with a firm banishing afterwards. I am told that the working was a great success and the benefits of it are still being enjoyed today for those whom it was worked for. For without doubt the mirror of arte is a useful and versatile magical tool which has not been fully realised by many students of the arte and I hope that this work will help to encourage others to explore it.

Elemental Invoking & Banishing Pentagrams

Invoking Pentagrams

Banishing Pentagrams

Further Reading

Liber Noctis - G. St. M. Nottingham (2004), Mercurius Press, Clun

Ars Salomonis - G. St. M. Nottingham (2011), Mercurius Press, Clun

Practical Candle Magic - M. A. Howard (2005), Ignotus Press

Practical Planetary Magick - David Rankine & Sorita d'Este (2007), Avalonia, London

Initiation into Hermetics - Franz Bardon (2013), Merkur Publishing, Salt Lake City

The Magus - Francis Barrett (2000, originally 1801), Red Wheel Weiser, Maine

The Art of Drawing Spirits into Crystals - Abbot Trithemius of Spanheim, available online at http://www.esotericarchives.com/tritheim/trchryst.htm

Liber Terribilis

Index

A

alchemy 14
Alice Through the Looking
 Glass 12
All Hallow Eve 12
aloes 19
Aquarius 38
Aral 30
Aries 40
Ars Geomantica 17
Ars Salomonis 23, 43

B

blue 31, 41

C

Cancer 21
candle ... 19, 27, 33, 36, 38, 40, 41
Canterbury Tales 11
catoptromancy 11
censer 21
Chassan 29
cord 24, 33, 35
crystal ball 16

D

dammar 29
Dee, Dr John 12
Djinn, King of Fire 30

dragon's blood 30

E

Earth 24, 25, 26, 31, 32, 33, 34, 36, 37
evil eye 12
eyebright 14

F

fluid condenser 16, 43
Fortune, Dion 15
frankincense 19, 21, 25

G

Gabriel, Archangel. 17, 21, 31
galbanum 29
Gemini 38
Ghob, King of Earth 26, 27, 32
gnomes 32
Goetia 44
green 14, 25, 26, 32, 36, 37

H

hazel 14

I

incense 17, 18, 19, 21, 24, 25, 33, 35, 39, 41
Initiation into Hermetics ... 43

Index

J

jasmine 19, 31
Jung, C.G. 14

K

Kelley, Edward 12

L

LBRP 17, 18, 21, 24, 25, 27, 35
Leo 40
Lesser Banishing Ritual of the Pentagram. 17, 24, See LBRP
Liber Noctis 17, 23, 43
Libra 38
ligature 33

M

Merlin 11
Mikael, Archangel 30
mirror 11, 12, 14, 15, 16, 17, 18, 19, 20, 21, 23, 24, 25, 26, 27, 33, 35, 36, 37, 38, 39, 40, 41, 42, 43, 44
mugwort 14, 16, 19
myrrh 33

N

Narcissus 12
nettle 30
Niksa, King of Water 31

P

Paralda, King of Air 29
patchouli 32
pepper 30
Phorlak 26, 27, 32
Pisces 21
Psalm 109 33

Psalm 126 36
Psalms 27
purple 17, 21

R

Raphael, Archangel 29
red 30
rose 31, 42

S

Sagittarius 40
salamanders 30
salt water 16
Scorpio 21
scriomancy 23
Seal of Solomon 44
Seere 44
shewstone. 12, 16, 17, 19, 21, 24, 25, 44
Snow White 12
Song of Solomon 41
spagyrics 14
storax 32
sylphs 29

T

Taliahad 31
Taurus 36

U

undines 31
Uriel, Archangel 25, 27, 32

V

vanilla 31
Vulcan 11

W

white 14, 17, 21, 25

white sandal 19

Y

yellow 29
Yesod 15, 17

FOUNDATIONS OF PRACTICAL SORCERY

A seven-volume set of magical treatises, unabridged, comprising:

Vol. I - Liber Noctis

A Handbook of the Sorcerous Arte

Liber Noctis explores the attitudes, training and preparation required for success in ritual, and, as the title suggests, does not shy away from the 'darker' aspects of magic. Practical, experiential, lucid and non-judgmental, this book lays the groundwork for the successful study and practice of sorcery in the modern world.

Vol. II - Ars Salomonis

Being of that Hidden Arte of Solomon the King

Ars Salomonis is a practical manual for working with the talismanic figures found in the Key of Solomon, the most significant of all grimoires. Including two methods for empowering and activating the planetary pentacles, the author makes this vital work safely accessible to beginners. It is an ideal entranceway into the grimoire tradition.

Vol. III - Ars Geomantica

Being an account and rendition of the Arte of Geomantic Divination and Magic

Ars Geomantica explores the medieval system of Geomancy, one of the simplest and most practical of the divinatory arts. The inclusion of detailed instructions on the creation of geomantic staves, elemental fluid condensers, and talismanic construction and consecration make this work a superb introduction to an extensive assortment of magical and divinatory principles.

Vol. IV - Ars Theurgia Goetia

Being an account and rendition of the Arte and Praxis of the Conjuration of some of the Spirits of Solomon

Ars Theurgia Goetia presents a precise and practical guide to working with the spirits of this neglected text from the Solomonic grimoire cycle, the Theurgia-Goetia, giving the full seals of the spirits for the first time. The complete ritual sequence of preparation, conjuration, and license to depart is lucidly demonstrated, making this work suitable for both the beginner and the experienced practitioner.

Vol. V - Otz Chim

The Tree of Life

Otz Chim is a practical exploration of the magic of the Kabbalistic Tree of Life, the glyph that concentrates the essence of magic and mysticism within the Western Mystery Tradition. This book focuses on lesser-known aspects such as the angels associated with the paths, their seals, and invocations and includes the previously unavailable Massa Aborum Vitae.

Vol. VI - Ars Speculum

Being an Instruction on the Arte of using Mirrors and Shewstones in Magic

Ars Speculum is a concise and practical work on the use of mirrors and shewstones in magic. In it the author explores skrying and working with the four elements of air, fire, water and earth - both with elemental condensers and different elemental creatures. Other techniques include contacting other levels of being, the conjuration of spirits, binding and ligature, and healing and protection.

Vol. VII - Liber Terriblis

Being an Instruction on the seventy-two Spirits of the Goetia

Liber Terribilis is a practical study of how to work with the seventy-two spirits of the infamous seventeenth-century Grimoire, the Goetia. It also explores the vital and often neglected use of the seventy-two binding angels of the Great Name of God, the Schemhamphorasch. This volume will be of value to all levels of students and practitioners of the grimoire traditions, being based upon the work of a small group of occultists who have explored it in practice.

More information available on the Avalonia website-
www.avaloniabooks.co.uk

Or write to:
BM Avalonia
London
WC1N 3XX
England, United Kingdom

Expanding the Esoteric Horizons ...

Avalonia *is an independent publisher producing outstanding and innovative books which push the boundaries of their subjects and illuminate the spirit of the sacred in its many manifestations.*

Explore some of the other works on the occult, mythology and magic published by Avalonia at:

www.avaloniabooks.co.uk

Readers who found Foundations of Practical Sorcery of interest, is likely to enjoy:

A Collection of Magical Secrets & a Treatise of mixed Cabalah by Stephen Skinner and David Rankine

Climbing the Tree of Life by David Rankine

Living Theurgy by Jeffrey S. Kupperman

Practical Elemental Magick by Sorita d'Este and David Rankine

The Book of Gold by David Rankine & Paul Harry Barron (trans.)

The Book of Treasure Spirits, edited by David Rankine

The Complete Grimoire of Pope Honorius by David Rankine & Paul Harry Barron (trans.)

The Cunning Man's Handbook by Jim Baker

The Grimoire of Arthur Gauntlet by David Rankine

Thoth by Lesley Jackson

Thracian Magic by Georgi Mishev

Wicca Magickal Beginnings by Sorita d'Este and David Rankine

www.ingramcontent.com/pod-product-compliance
Lightning Source LLC
LaVergne TN
LVHW091552070426
835507LV00010B/809